Amazonia

Susan Powell and Rose Inserra

Heinemann
LIBRARY

©1997 Ogma Writers

Published by Heinemann Library

an imprint of Reed Educational & Professional Publishing

500 Coventry Lane

Crystal Lake, IL 60014

Library of Congress Cataloging-in-Publication Data

Powell, Susan, 1942-

    Amazonia / Susan Powell and Rose Inserra.

      p. cm. -- (Ends of the earth)

    Includes index.

    Summary: Describes the geography, wildlife, and people of the Amazon River and its drainage basin.

    ISBN 0-431-06935. 2 (lib. bdg.)

    1. Amazon River Region--Description and travel--Juvenile literature. 2. Natural history--Amazon River Region--Juvenile literature. 3. Nature--Effect of human beings on--Amazon River Region--Juvenile literature. [1. Amazon River Region. 2. Natural history--Amazon River Region. 3. Nature--Effect of human beings on--Amazon River Region.] I. Inserra, Rose, 1958- . II. Title. III. Series.

F2546.P8545 1997

981'.1--dc21

                                                97-1927

                                                  CIP

                                                      AC

01 00 99 98 97

10 9 8 7 6 5 4 3 2 1

Designed by David Doyle and Irwin Liaw

Edited by Ogma Writers and Editors

Front and back cover photographs courtesy of André Bärtschi

Picture research by Ogma Writers and Editors

Illustrations by Andrew Plant

Cartography by Ophelia Leviny

Production by Elena Cementon

Printed in Hong Kong by H&Y Printing Limited

Contents

Part 1 The Beginning

Amazonia	4
The amazing Amazon	6
In the beginning	8
Journey along the Amazon	10

Part 2 Inside the Rainforest

Tropical rainforests	12
Wildlife of the Amazon	14
Birds of the forest	16
Case study: two Amazonian reptiles	18
The generous forest	20
The vanishing rainforest	22

Part 3 People of the Rainforest

Indians of the Amazon	24
Farming the forest	26
Spirits and shamans	28
Age of the conquistadors	30
Orellana's journey	32
The "new world"	34

Part 4 A Developing World

The rubber revolution	36
Four Amazonian towns	38
Amazonians today	40
Industries in Amazonia	42
Fightback and the future	44
The message	46
Glossary	47
Index	48

Amazonia

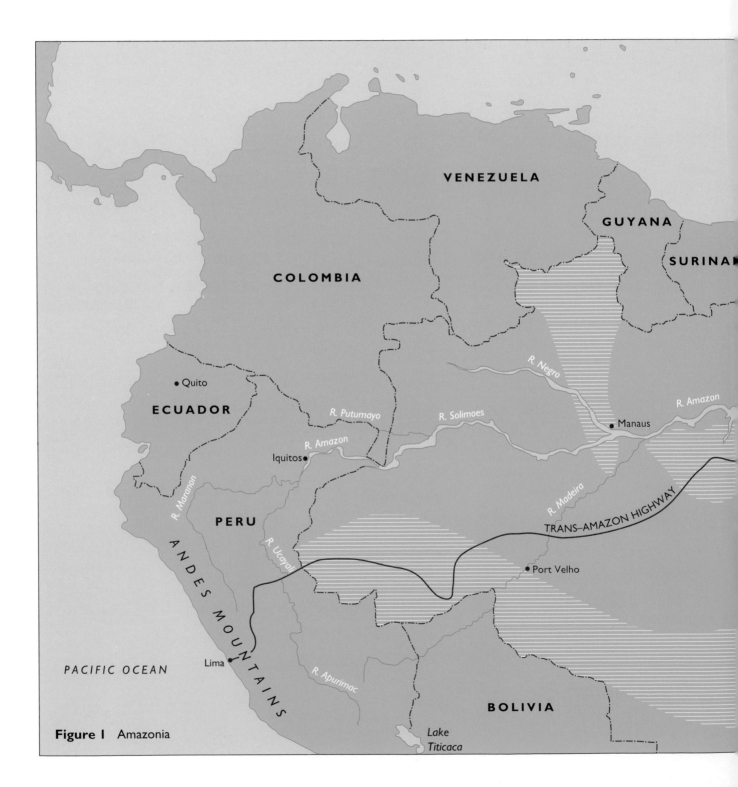

PACIFIC OCEAN

Figure 1 Amazonia

The Amazon River and its huge basin are among the greatest creations of nature. Amazonia, the name by which the river and its basin are known, is also one of the most interesting areas of the world to read about. History and geography come alive along this extensive waterway, which in places behaves like a sea, and has so many tributaries that they are almost beyond counting.

Amazonia is an environment quite unlike any other. The rainforests that cover much of the region are renowned for their beauty and their abundant and unusual species of plants and animals. The forest is also important as the home of the remaining groups of Amazon Indians. These traditional inhabitants are today greatly outnumbered by the many other groups of settlers attempting to make a living in the Amazon Basin.

In one sense Amazonia is at the ends of the Earth, yet its fate is relevant to people everywhere. This book examines the mighty river system and the life it supports, and discusses why this very special environment needs to be protected.

Amazonia's variety

Although Amazonia is most famous for its rainforest, the region also features other forms of vegetation. There are cool and misty forests (in the west), swampy mangroves (in the east), areas of small twisted trees and grasslands (in the south), and savanna (in the north).

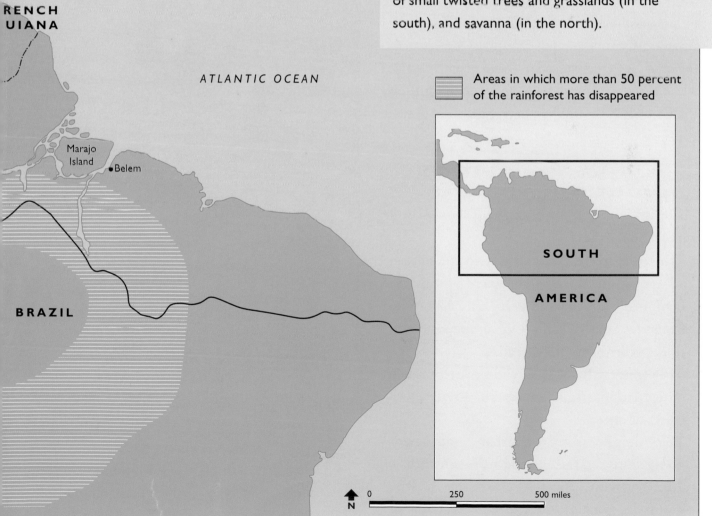

Areas in which more than 50 percent of the rainforest has disappeared

FRENCH GUIANA

ATLANTIC OCEAN

Marajo Island

Belem

BRAZIL

SOUTH

AMERICA

0   250   500 miles

N

The amazing Amazon

Where on Earth...?

Eleven countries lie within the continent of South America. Brazil is by far the largest, followed in size by Argentina. The fifth largest country in the world, Brazil has a population of 148,000,000 people. Its capital is Brasilia.

The Amazon Basin dominates the northern part of the country. Most of the countries surrounding Brazil—Peru, Bolivia, French Guiana, Surinam, Guyana, Venezuela, Ecuador, Colombia, and Paraguay—are part of the river system too, or are influenced by it. In all, Amazonia covers two and a half million square miles—more than half the area of South America.

What's so amazing about the Amazon?

There is a number of reasons why the Amazon River is so special.

- The rivers in the Amazon system run almost all the way across the continent—from the heights of the Andes in Peru, only 125 miles from the South Pacific Ocean, across Brazil to the North Atlantic Ocean.

- The Amazon River is so wide that for much of its length it is impossible to see both banks at once.

- The Amazon is so deep that huge ocean-going ships can travel along half its length.

- Together with 1100 tributaries, the Amazon drains an area almost the size of Australia, or

(Photo courtesy of Adventure World)

ten times the size of France.

- Due to the types of rock over which they flow, rivers in the system appear to be different colors. At one point, two colors flow separately along the same stretch of river.

- The world's largest tropical rainforest lies in Amazonia. Within the forest are hundreds of thousands of plant and animal species, many

Figure 3 (right)   No bridge crosses the mighty Amazon for more than 3850 miles. With its complex system of tributaries, the Amazon drains more than half of South America.

Figure 2 (below)   The leaves of the giant waterlily can grow to almost 7 feet in diameter. Its large white flowers have been known to reach the size of a human head.

Figure 4 (above)   At 3900 miles, the Amazon is not quite the longest river in the world. That distinction goes to the Nile in Egypt, which is 4145 miles long. The Amazon, however, carries much more water than the Nile. What we call the Amazon is actually a main river fed by many other rivers, some of which originate in the countries surrounding Brazil. Some of these rivers, which are major waterways in themselves, are more than 990 miles in length. The Madeira River that originates in Bolivia is the longest at 1987 miles.

of them found nowhere else on Earth.

- Up to 200,000 of the remaining indigenous people of Amazonia, known as Indians, still live in the region of their ancestors.
- The Amazon Basin is one of the wettest areas in the world, averaging more than 100 inches of rainfall a year.
- The Amazon region is home to 2500 kinds of fish (nearly ten times the number found in Europe) and 30,000 kinds of flowering plants (one-third of the total found in South America and nearly three times the number in Europe).
- Among the amazing variety of plants found in the Amazon region is a giant waterlily which grows up to 7 feet wide.

In the beginning

Hundreds of millions of years ago, the Earth's land masses were joined together into two huge supercontinents. Scientists refer to the southern one as Gondwana. When this super-continent gradually started to break apart about 180 million years ago, it split into five continents, one of which became South America. Just inland from the Pacific Ocean, in what is today Peru, the Andes Mountains began to rise. These mountains prevented the formation of a river that would flow west into the Pacific Ocean. Instead, inland water was trapped in a huge lake. Eventually, fed by hundreds of mountain streams, the lake grew into a river which ran east to the Atlantic coast: that river was the Amazon.

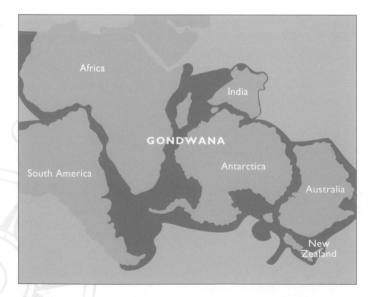

Passage to Amazonia

It is thought that the indigenous people of Amazonia could have been living in the rain-forest for 20,000 years; some experts even put the figure at 50,000 years. This race of people, called "Indians" by early European explorers, originally came from Central Asia. Crossing the Bering Strait to Alaska, they slowly trav-eled through what are now Canada, the United States of America and Mexico to settle in Central and South America.

It has not been easy for scientists to piece together the history of the Indians because parts of Amazonia are so inaccessible. On top of this, the Indians lead simple lives with few possessions, and frequently move from place to place. This has meant that clues from their past are quickly erased by the growth of the forest or by the heavy rain and high humidity. All that remain of the long-ago dwellers of the forest are some burial mounds made of shells, some stone hammers, and fragments of pottery.

Figure 5 (left) The supercontinent of Gondwana consisted of South America, Africa, India, Antarctica, and Australasia. During the Triassic period millions of years ago, Africa and South America began to separate and form the continents that we know today.

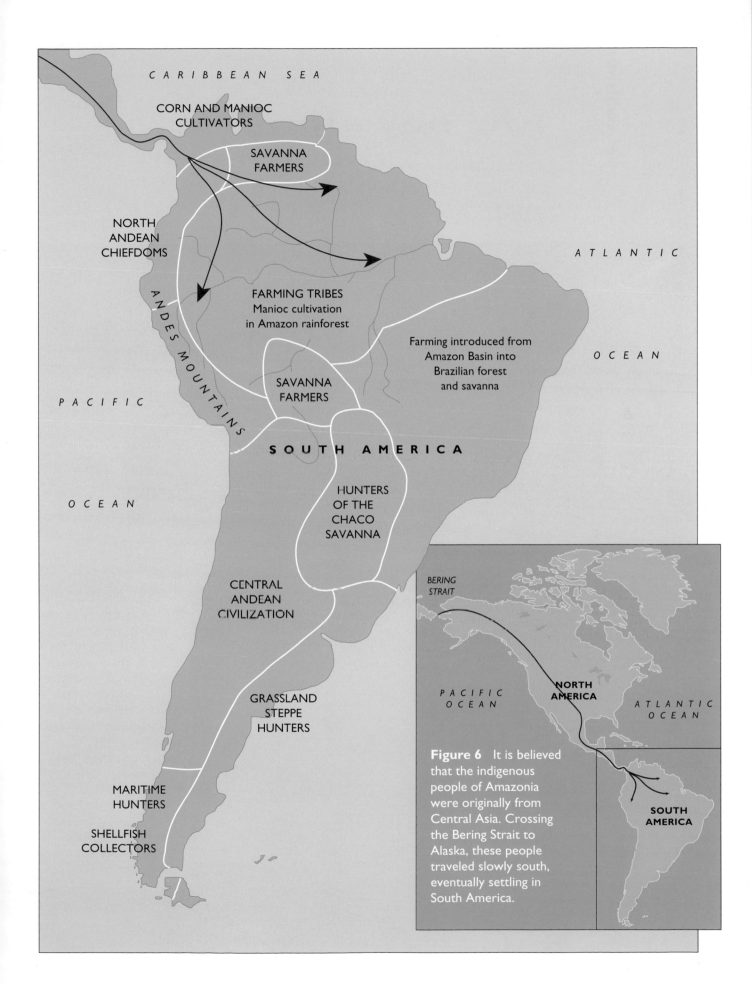

CARIBBEAN SEA

CORN AND MANIOC CULTIVATORS

SAVANNA FARMERS

NORTH ANDEAN CHIEFDOMS

ANDES MOUNTAINS

FARMING TRIBES
Manioc cultivation in Amazon rainforest

Farming introduced from Amazon Basin into Brazilian forest and savanna

ATLANTIC

OCEAN

PACIFIC

SAVANNA FARMERS

SOUTH AMERICA

OCEAN

HUNTERS OF THE CHACO SAVANNA

CENTRAL ANDEAN CIVILIZATION

GRASSLAND STEPPE HUNTERS

MARITIME HUNTERS

SHELLFISH COLLECTORS

BERING STRAIT

PACIFIC OCEAN

NORTH AMERICA

ATLANTIC OCEAN

Figure 6 It is believed that the indigenous people of Amazonia were originally from Central Asia. Crossing the Bering Strait to Alaska, these people traveled slowly south, eventually settling in South America.

SOUTH AMERICA

Journey along the Amazon

B As the mountains flatten out, the river slows down considerably and starts to flow eastward across the great plain of Brazil. The temperature rises and with it the rainfall.

COLOMBIA

VENEZU

Quito

ECUADOR

R. Napo

PLAIN

R. Japura

R. Amazon

R. Solimoes

C

Iquitos

BRAZIL

B

R. Maranon

R. Ucayali

PERU

PACIFIC
OCEAN

ANDES MOUNTAINS

C By this stage the waterway is already twice the width of the Rhine, the largest river in Europe. Even before it leaves Peru, it has had several name changes: the Apurimac, the Ene, the Tombo, the Ucayali, and finally the Amazon as the river enters Brazil. Later still it is called the Solimoes, becoming the Amazon again where it meets the Rio Negro.

R. Tombo

A It is in Peru, less than 125 miles from the Pacific coast, that the Amazon has its beginnings. It starts as a very small stream high in the Andes Mountains, where the air is very cold. Little grows except stunted trees and grasses. Here the waters from glaciers run down into lakes; from these lakes flow streams that carve a steep path downhill, passing through beautiful gorges and over rapids. These streams eventually join the fast-flowing Apurimac River, which churns up clay as it goes, turning its waters a milky coffee or yellow color.

R. Ene

R. Apurimac

BOLIVIA

A

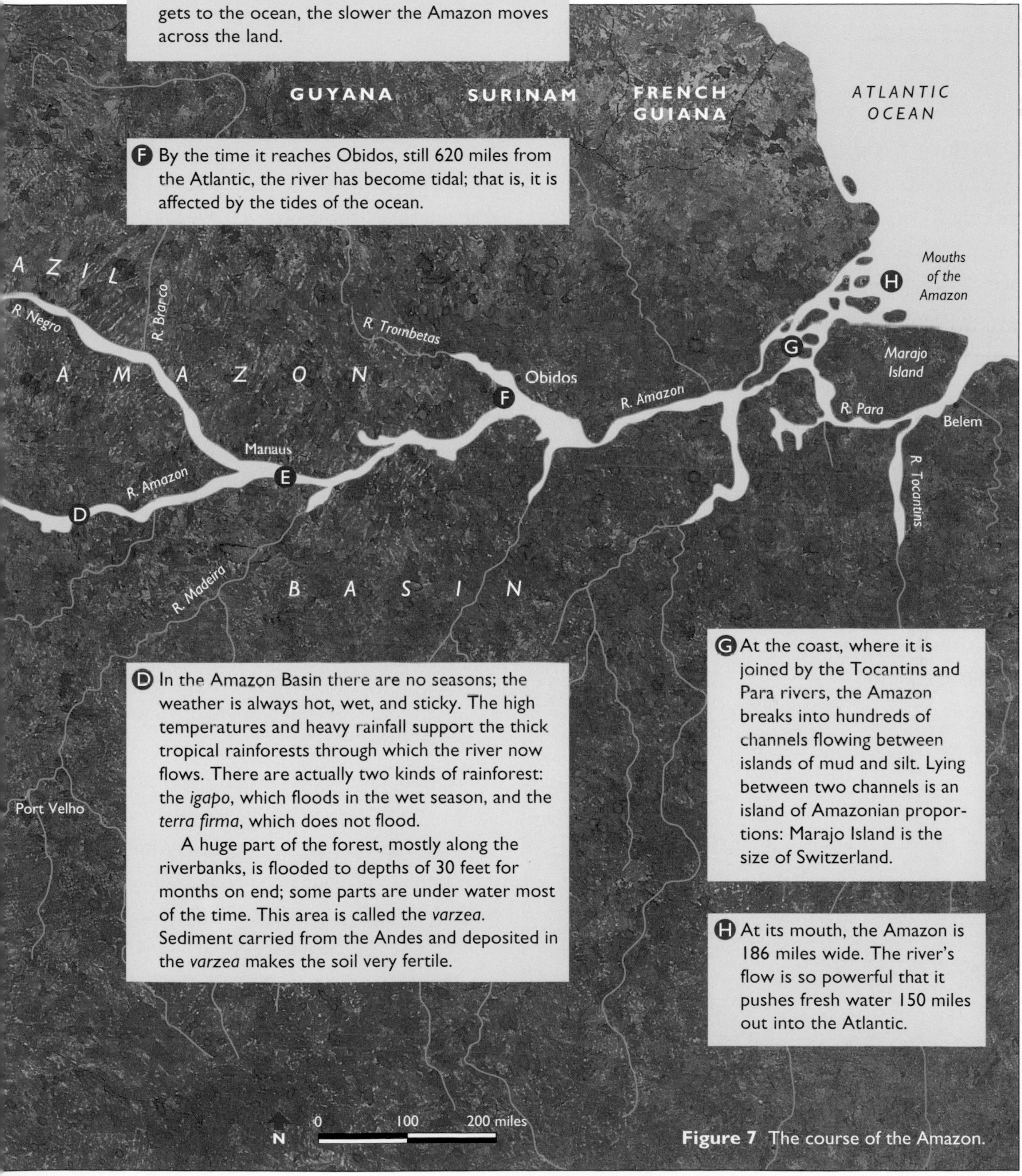

E The Amazon Basin is flat; hardly any ground is more than 600 feet above sea level. The closer it gets to the ocean, the slower the Amazon moves across the land.

GUYANA   SURINAM   FRENCH GUIANA   *ATLANTIC OCEAN*

F By the time it reaches Obidos, still 620 miles from the Atlantic, the river has become tidal; that is, it is affected by the tides of the ocean.

BRAZIL

R. Negro *R. Branco* *R. Trombetas*

Mouths of the Amazon

H

G

Marajo Island

A M A Z O N

Obidos

F

R. Amazon

R. Para

Belem

Manaus

E

R. Amazon

D

R. Tocantins

R. Madeira   B A S I N

Port Velho

D In the Amazon Basin there are no seasons; the weather is always hot, wet, and sticky. The high temperatures and heavy rainfall support the thick tropical rainforests through which the river now flows. There are actually two kinds of rainforest: the *igapo*, which floods in the wet season, and the *terra firma*, which does not flood.

A huge part of the forest, mostly along the riverbanks, is flooded to depths of 30 feet for months on end; some parts are under water most of the time. This area is called the *varzea*. Sediment carried from the Andes and deposited in the *varzea* makes the soil very fertile.

G At the coast, where it is joined by the Tocantins and Para rivers, the Amazon breaks into hundreds of channels flowing between islands of mud and silt. Lying between two channels is an island of Amazonian proportions: Marajo Island is the size of Switzerland.

H At its mouth, the Amazon is 186 miles wide. The river's flow is so powerful that it pushes fresh water 150 miles out into the Atlantic.

N   0   100   200 miles

Figure 7 The course of the Amazon.

Tropical rainforests

What is a rainforest?

A rainforest is far more than a collection of trees growing closely together. Rainforests are unique combinations of plants and animals which depend on, and contribute to, one another. This interdependence is called an ecosystem.

Tropical rainforests consist of several layers of vegetation, each layer an ideal habitat for the particular plants and animals that exist within it. Everything in the forest depends on something else. Tall trees provide dappled sunlight and shade for smaller trees, and direct the rain down their tipped, waxy leaves to the plants below. At a lower level, tree trunks and branches support vines, creepers and epiphytes (plants which grow on other plants, but do not rely on them for food). This enclosed world creates just the right amount of humidity for its inhabitants.

Birds and animals play a role in pollinating plants and spreading their seeds; at the same time, the plants provide shelter and food for the birds and animals. Even insects have a role; they break down the waste matter on the forest floor, and turn it into compost to feed the plants. Take away any one of these "players" and the whole delicate balance is upset.

(Photo courtesy of André Bärtschi)

Figure 8

Emergent trees

The majority of tall rainforest trees—hardwoods like mahogany, brazil nut and silk cotton—have shallow, wide-spreading roots just beneath the soil surface. These roots enable the trees to take up all available moisture and nutrients. This type of root system also holds the soil together, a fact that becomes obvious when rainforests are cleared and the soil is easily washed away.

Occasionally, single trees can be seen poking out above the canopy. Soaring up to 200 feet high, these are known as emergent trees. The reason they can achieve such great heights is that they are buttressed (held up) by special roots which grow stilt-like above the ground.

Figure 9
Creatures of the rainforest

Harpy eagle

Spider monkey

Toucan

Scarlet macaw

Ornate umbrella bird

Hyacinthine macaw

Ocelot

Topaz humming bird

Sloth

Tamandua

Cotton headed tamarin

Iguana

Kinkajou

Porcupine

Scarlet tanager

Coati

Hoatzin

Anaconda

Tapir

Giant anteater

Giant armadillo

Capybara

Emergent trees

Canopy

Understory

Floor

Figure 10
The parts of the rainforest

Canopy
The forest's top layer, called the canopy, rises up to above the ground. This layer is where the crowns of the highest trees are found. Because the canopy receives the most rain and sun, it supports more life than the rest of the forest. Birds such as eagles, parrots, macaws, and toucans; tropical bats; insects; and many types of monkeys and sloths all live in the canopy.

Understory
Beneath the canopy is the humid understory. Here it is darker and gloomier among the shorter trees, ferns, shrubs, palms, and young saplings that do not require as much sun and water. Thick lianas and other creepers which enjoy the filtered light entwine themselves around branches.

Floor
The forest floor receives only 5 percent of the sunlight that falls on the canopy; only those plants which can cope with the almost total lack of light can survive. Mammals such as the long-nosed tapir make their home here, as do capybaras (the world's largest rodents), armadillos, jaguars, pumas, and giant toads.

Humus (rotting leaves, fallen branches and other organic matter) lies on the ground, providing a habitat for thousands of species of insects, small animals, and fungi. This material decomposes rapidly in the hot, damp conditions and produces minerals which are taken up by the tree roots.

Wildlife of the Amazon

The Amazon River supports a fascinating variety of animal life. It is home to almost one in five of all the bird species on Earth, and more than one in ten of all animal species.

Giant fish: the pirarucu

One of the world's largest freshwater fish, the pirarucu, is found in the waters of the Amazon. More than 10 feet in length and weighing a mammoth 440 pounds, the pirarucu is also known for its tongue-bite. Most fish bite with teeth set into their jaws; the pirarucu, however, bites with teeth that line its tongue. Indians have dried these tongues and used them to grate seeds for mixing into drinks.

Electric eel

The Amazonian electric eel has an unusual feature—its "lung" is located inside its mouth. The eel's mouth is lined with sacs that take in oxygen which is then transported to the body tissues along the blood vessels. While most animals carry blood containing oxygen in their arteries and deoxygenated blood in their veins, these eels transport both mixed together. Because of this mixing, which reduces the blood's oxygen-giving quality, the eel must surface every 2–3 minutes to take in more oxygen.

To protect its "lung" from being damaged while catching food, the electric eel shocks its prey with an electric charge of 300 to 500 volts, making sure its victim's death-struggle is brief. Amazonian legends claim that the eels also use this electric charge to shake fruit from the assai tree. Apparently the eel coils itself around the trunk and then sends a shock up the stem, causing the tree to drop its fruit.

Capybara: world's largest rodent

Amazonia is also host to the world's largest rodent (the family that also includes rats and guinea-pigs). The capybara can weigh up to 145 pounds. Capybara is an Indian name meaning "master of the grasses," which

Figure 11 (left) Amazonian children become familiar with a wide range of wildlife at an early age.

(Photo courtesy of Destination Holidays)

Figure 13 (below) Capybaras have a well-developed sense of smell, which is useful in identifying the different scent of each member of the group.

Figure 12 (above) With the ease of a gymnast, this monkey swings itself from vine to vine. There are about 40 species of monkeys in the Amazon Basin alone.

describes the feeding habits of these unusual animals. The bulk of their diet consists of grasses floating in the river channels, but some types of capybara are also known to eat leaves off trees. Capybaras live in groups of up to 15; they usually spend their day resting in the morning, bathing at midday, then eating heavily through the late afternoon and night.

In Venezuela in the 1500s, some Catholic monks decided that the animals were fish, and could therefore be eaten when other meats were banned by certain religious observances.

Other fascinating facts

Among its incredible collection of wildlife, the Amazon also boasts:

- a species of catfish weighing up to 400 pounds
- the smallest monkey in the world—the pygmy marmoset—which weighs an average of four and a half ounces
- the arowhana fish, which jumps out of the water to snatch spiders and insects off overhanging branches
- dolphins and more than 20 species of stingrays swimming in its massive river system
- a type of sea cow known as a manatee, which continually sheds its old teeth and replaces them with new ones grown at the back of its mouth.

Birds of the forest

In contrast with the dense green foliage of the Amazon rainforests are its brilliantly colored birds. There are almost 900 species found in the Amazon Basin—one-tenth of the world's total.

Toucans

The toucan is one of Amazonia's most well-known birds. It has a huge beak that looks as if it requires all the bird's strength to support it. In fact it is made of a light substance supported by a web of bones and tissues. In some species, this brightly-colored bill is longer than the bird's body.

(Photo courtesy of Destination Holidays)

Unlike macaws, which prefer a diet of seeds, toucans could be called "seed-spitters," as they prefer to feed only on the flesh of fruit. The bird's colorful beak is serrated like a knife, for breaking open the fruit. Its feathers are a combination of black, blue, green, brown, yellow, and red and make a spectacular addition to the forest.

Macaws

While toucans are recognized by their enormous beaks, the birds known as macaws are recognized by their long tail feathers. Of the 17 known species of macaw in South America, those found in the Amazon region have unusual habits which make good use of the rainforest and river.

With predators always on the hunt for a meal, it is dangerous for macaws to sleep in the same place as they eat. To prevent predators finding their nests, the macaws fly across the river to feed each morning, then return to the trees on the opposite bank to sleep at night.

In addition to eating seeds (which they clamp between their feet and break open with their beaks), macaws also eat soil and pebbles. The pebbles help them to grind their food, making it easier to digest, while the soil adds mineral salts to their diet.

Figure 14 (left)   Another bird known for its massive beak is the jabiru stork. It feeds in shallow waters on a diet including large fish, turtles, and young caiman.

(Photo courtesy of André Bärtschi)

Figure 15 (below)   This blue and yellow macaw is perched in a brazil nut tree, extracting the nuts from the unripe fruit pods.

(Photo courtesy of the Brazilian Tourist Office)

Figure 16 (above) Some scientists believe that the bright coloring of the toucan's beak may act as a warning: "beware or I'll bite."

Threats

Unfortunately, the survival of these spectacular birds is under threat. In 1992, the International Council for Bird Preservation listed Brazil as having the second highest number of threatened species of birds in the world. In addition to the destruction of their natural habitat and poisoning from pollution, the species are also under threat from poachers. The beautiful Amazonian birds can be sold for high prices in the illegal bird trade. However, once they are removed from their spacious natural environment and placed in cages, the captured birds are unlikely to survive.

Colors of the birds: an Indian legend

One Indian legend describes how the birds acquired their colored feathers.

Threatened by a fearsome water snake which was killing hundreds of creatures, the Indians and birds decided to combine forces. However, it was the brave cormorant that dived into the water and fatally wounded the snake. Once the Indians had skinned the creature, the cormorant asked for his trophy. To the Indians' dismay, all the birds swooped down and flew off with the snake skin in their beaks.

Agreeing to share their prize, each bird claimed whatever section it held in its beak. Miraculously, the red, yellow, green, black, and white pattern on each section of the skin transferred itself to their feathers. The cormorant, however, was holding the dark head of the snake skin and was turned black, a color he thought acceptable for an old bird like himself.

Case study: two Amazonian reptiles

The anaconda

Among the amazing wildlife found in the Amazon region is the world's largest and heaviest snake. *Eunectes murinus*, more commonly known as the anaconda, is a species that grows to an average length of 20 feet, but has been known to reach more than 32 feet in length with a weight of up to 550 pounds.

Unlike venomous snakes which kill their victims with poison, the anaconda is a constrictor. A constrictor coils itself around its victim and slowly tightens its grip each time its prey breathes out. Once dead, the unfortunate animal is swallowed whole and slowly digested.

Explorers, prospectors, scientists, and others traveling through the Amazon sometimes crossed the anaconda's path. In 1923, in *Head Hunters of the Amazon*, Fritz W. Up de Graff wrote:

> *There lay in the mud and water, covered with flies, butterflies, and insects ... the most colossal anaconda ... Ten or twelve feet of it lay stretched out on the bank in the mud. The rest of it lay in the clear shallow water ... its body as thick as a man's waist ... How utterly helpless the mightiest of men would be in the coils of such a monster!*

Figure 17 (right) Anacondas spend much of their time in the water, waiting to catch mammals and birds which come to drink. They are also known to eat turtles, fish, and even small caimans.

Unfortunately, the anaconda is now under threat from the interference of local human settlements. As for other species, regulations need to be introduced and enforced to protect this unique Amazonian snake.

The caiman

Several species of caiman, members of the Alligatoridae family, are found in the Amazon region.

Figure 18
(left) In South America, all alligatorids are known as caimans. The largest, the black caiman, can grow to more than 20 feet in length.

The common caiman is the world's most hunted species of alligator, representing 60 to 80 percent of the world's skin trade.

At least two species of dwarf caiman are found in Amazonia, mainly concentrated in the thick rainforests. They have a strange armor formed by a buildup of calcium in the tissue under the skin's surface. Another unusual feature of the dwarf caiman is its eyes: most other crocodilians have yellow eyes, but the dwarf caiman's are a deep brown color.

Unfortunately for the black caiman, *Melanosuchus niger*, it has no bony lumps on its belly, making its skin very valuable to hunters. In the 1950s and 1960s, the demand for these skins to produce luxury items such as handbags drastically reduced the black caiman population.

The generous forest

The Amazon rainforest is important to the many animals, plants, and people that make it their home. However it is also important in other ways to people all over the world, and to the general "health" of the planet.

The lungs of the Earth

Trees (and other plants) carry out a function that is vital to life on Earth—photosynthesis. The green substance in a tree's leaves (called chlorophyll) uses the energy in sunlight to convert carbon dioxide from the atmosphere into carbohydrates. These carbohydrates provide food for the tree. As a by-product of this process, the tree gives out oxygen and moisture. In this way, trees help to "cleanse" the air, reducing the amount of carbon dioxide in the atmosphere. In the Amazon rainforest, this happens on a huge scale.

Cutting down forest trees means this "cleansing" of the air cannot take place; in addition, burning the trees releases large amounts of stored up carbon dioxide back into the atmosphere.

(Photo courtesy of Peregrine Adventure)

Figure 19 (right) Each year, Western countries import thousands of tons of rainforest plants (such as the leaves of the rosy periwinkle, shown here) to be made into medicinal drugs such as muscle relaxants, cancer drugs, and contraceptives.

Figure 20 (below)   By its sheer size, the Amazonian rainforest plays an important role in absorbing carbon dioxide from the Earth's atmosphere.

Figure 21 (above)   Cotton grows wild in the Amazon rainforest, and is also cultivated by some Indian groups.

Healing plants

For thousands of years, indigenous people around the world have been experts in the use of rainforest plants for healing purposes. Plants, they long ago discovered, were useful for treating many of their common ailments.

Today, Western countries import thousands of tons of rainforest plants to be made into medicinal drugs to treat conditions ranging from heart disease and cancer, to infec- tious diseases and mental illness. They are also used in contraceptives, muscle relaxants, anti- histamines, and anesthetics. For example, the leaves of the rosy periwinkle have been success- ful in the treatment of Hodgkin's disease and childhood leukaemia, and the bark of the cin- chona tree produces quinine, which is used to treat malaria. In fact, perhaps a quarter of the goods we buy in drugstores, from soaps to medicines, contain an ingredient that comes from species found in rainforests.

So huge and dense is the Amazon rainforest that large parts of it have not yet been fully explored. Scientists have still to examine and classify much of its flora and fauna. New uses are continually being found for rainforest plants, and there are great hopes that they will yield cures to some of our more serious diseases.

The vanishing rainforest

The world's tropical rainforests grow in a wide band that straddles the equator. This pattern of vegetation once covered some 12 percent of the Earth's surface. Today it covers about 7 percent. Nearly half of the Earth's rainforests have been cut down in the last 50 years for the timber they contain, and also to make way for other commercial activities such as farming and mining.

Figure 22 (below)   Some rainforest trees are cut down to be sold as timber, but many others are simply felled and burned to clear land for cattle grazing.

Rainforests change naturally: fire, disease, floods, and volcanoes all cause damage. However, these changes usually occur slowly, over thousands of years. By contrast, human activities have a much more devastating effect. It is estimated that an area of rainforest the size of several football fields is cleared every day. One-quarter of Brazil's rainforest has already disappeared. The total area of rainforest left in the world is now about the size of the United States of America.

(Photo courtesy of André Bärtschi)

Appearances are deceiving

The appearance of rainforests can be misleading. While they may look dense and healthy, their ecosystems actually depend on fragile relationships. Disturb the connection between vegetation, soil, animals, climate, and other factors, and the rainforest cannot sustain itself.

It is not the soil that supports the rainforest. The poor, thin soil that is typical of tropical rainforests is just one factor in a complicated inter-relationship. The rainforest trees actually obtain their nutrients from the rich layer of humus (rotting plant material) that covers the forest floor.

When tall rainforest trees are cleared, the smaller plants that need shade and dappled sunlight wither. Animals and birds, deprived of their food sources and customary shelter, die out or move away. With the forest gone, the bare, exposed soil turns to dust. Heavy rains wash the soil, along with any remaining minerals and seeds, into the rivers. Silting up of the rivers causes the flooding of crops and villages.

(Photo courtesy of Destination Holidays)

Figure 24 (above) Although its soil is poor in nutrients, the Amazon region is still capable of supporting an incredible variety of plant and animal life. This is partly due to the complex ecosystem of the rainforest which is sometimes called a "nutrient reservoir."

The world's weather can also be affected if too much rainforest is removed. With fewer trees and more human activities that add carbon dioxide to the atmosphere, there is a danger of global warming (the gradual heating up of the planet). This could lead to floods and droughts, and to rising sea levels.

23

Indians of the Amazon

Before European settlement in the 1500s, Central and South America were inhabited by many related but distinct groups of people. The Europeans referred to them as "Indians." In some regions, these people built great civilizations, such as the Incas who lived in what is now Peru, and the Aztecs who inhabited present-day Mexico. The Amazonian Indians, however, have always lived simply, understanding and respecting their environment. To the Indians, the Amazon River system is a lifeline, providing a means of transport, a source of water for drinking and washing, and a source of fish for food. The forest provided them with food, shelter, medicine, and clothing.

It is estimated that several hundred years ago there were more than five million Amazonian Indians in more than 200 groups living in this way. Today there are between 100,000 and 200,000 who follow a traditional lifestyle. They are increasingly likely to make use of plastic or aluminum implements and manufactured clothing from the outside world.

Figure 25 Various types of shelters used by Indians in the Brazilian Amazon.

Families

For Amazonian Indians, the "family" includes even very distant relatives. These extended families usually live together, in one big, open house. Within the family, men and women have different roles. The women are responsible for tending and harvesting the crops, cooking most of the meals, and providing water. The men hunt, clear, and prepare the ground for planting, and do some of the outdoor cooking.

Children are given a lot of attention, and from an early age are encouraged to learn survival skills, such as hunting, using a bow and arrow, and throwing a spear, by watching and copying the adults. Everyone works together for the good of the group, and the children know what is expected of them from an early age.

When they reach puberty, young Indians go through coming-of-age ceremonies, which are a sign that they are entering adulthood. These initiation rites vary from group to group, and are different for boys and girls. They are often

Figure 26 (below) The Amazonian Indians use the many rivers in the region as if they were roads. They travel the waterways on a variety of crafts, including rafts, dugout canoes, and bark canoes.

Figure 27 (above)   A village of the Yagua Indians in the rainforest of Colombia. Because of the climate, Indians in the tropical rainforest wear few clothes. What coverings they do wear are generally made from cotton, which grows wild, as well as being cultivated. Cotton is also used for making hammocks. Some tribes make cloth from bark and other forest materials.

painful. After their initiation, the young people are expected to take part in the day-to-day activities of the group, and are able to marry.

Houses

Indian dwellings are usually made of wood and thatch, fixed with strips of bark, lengths of vine, or wooden nails. The shape of the house and the materials used vary according to the group's traditions and its surroundings, but they are all designed to let in the air and keep out the rain. There is generally a hole in the roof to let out smoke if cooking is done inside. There is little furniture and hammocks take the place of beds.

In the northwest of Amazonia, groups of up to 200 people may live together in houses called *malocas*. These structures have no internal walls: each family has a part of the building for their hammocks and possessions.

Members of another group, the Kayapo of Central Brazil, arrange their houses around a large central area. At the back are huts in which they do their cooking. A larger hut is built in the middle of the square for men to gather in and for ceremonial purposes.

Farming the forest

Slash and burn

The Indians have traditionally practiced a system of agriculture known as the "slash and burn" method. While it may sound destructive, it actually has many advantages and does no permanent harm to the rainforest.

Slash and burn is a method of shifting cultivation that is ideal in areas where the soil is poor. A group will select a piece of forest close to their village and cut down the large trees. The stumps and remaining vegetation are set on fire to clear the ground. The Indians do not clear more ground than they need because they know that the rain will wash away the soil if it is not protected.

The Indians then plant their crops, which are fertilized by the nutrients in the wood ash. Fruit trees are sometimes planted, not only for their fruit but also because they attract animals. The animals provide a source of food, and their droppings spread seeds.

After several harvests the soil is no longer fertile, so the Indians move to a new area of the forest and begin again. Forest plants soon take root in the abandoned clearing, and it slowly returns to its natural state.

Crops

In the high Andes mountains where the Amazon River starts, the Indians grow corn, potatoes, and a few other vegetables on the slopes. They raise llamas for their meat and also for yarn which they use to make clothing, since the weather here can be cold.

In the Amazon Basin the staple crop is a vegetable called manioc or cassava; its pulp is dried and mixed with water to make loaves that look like pancakes. The Indians also grow corn, yams, peanuts, and bananas. From the forest they gather berries and fruits, nuts, wild honey, and spices.

Their varied diet includes fish caught from the rivers using bow and arrow, nets, traps, or poison. Small animals, including wild pigs, rodents (such as agouti and paca), and tapirs, are caught by the same means.

(Photo courtesy of Adventure World)

Figure 28 This Indian woman is using new and traditional implements to make cassava pulp, which will then be baked into loaves.

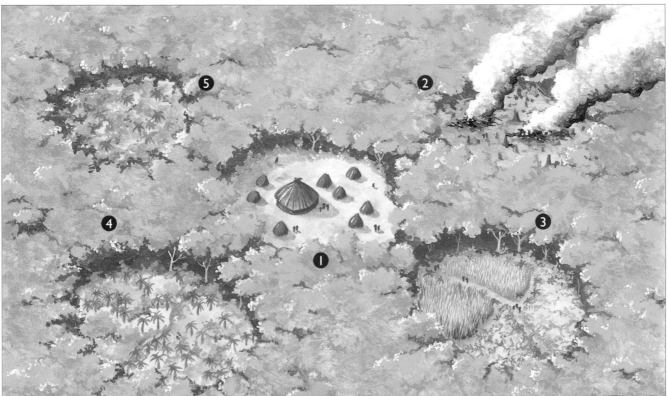

(Photo courtesy of Andre Bärtschi)

Figure 29 (above)   An Indian village usually has several gardens, each at a different stage of growth. The people of this village (1) have just cut a new garden (2). Garden (3) is already one year old and almost all the crops are ready for harvesting. Garden (4) is over two years old and is dominated by banana trees. Garden (5) is an old one which the Indians abandoned after about three years. This was so that the forest could reclaim it before its soil became exhausted.

Figure 30 (right)   The Indians of the Amazon are well known for their skill at hunting, especially with bows and arrows. Some tribes dip the arrowheads in poison juice extracted from the bark of the tiki uba tree. Other groups kill their prey using blowpipes made from bamboo, from which they shoot darts dipped in snake venom or curare. Curare is a plant extract that paralyses the muscles of its victims, eventually causing death.

An Indian barbecue
During the dry season, the rivers of the Amazon are at their lowest. The Indians take advantage of this by dropping certain crushed herbs into the river. These herbs drug the fish, bringing them to the surface where they drift downstream. The Indians trap the fish in a net made of braided reeds. The fish are then cured and stored for the wet season when meat is scarce. The fish are cooked on a rack which the Haitian Indians call a *barboka*. The Spanish borrowed this word as *barbacoa*—the ancestor of the modern barbecue.

Spirits and shamans

To the Indians, the rainforest is not just a place to live and a source of food. It is also the sacred home of the spirits which they believe inhabit every living thing and guide them in their everyday lives. Many of the spirits are believed to be powerful and dangerous, capable of causing illness, bad luck, and even death.

Shamans are special individuals (always males) who can communicate with these spirits. The main task of the shamans is to heal, and they do this by using their contact with the spirit world as well as their wide knowledge of rainforest plants. The shamans are thought to be able to cure illnesses by "sucking out" the invisible objects that the spirits have "blown" into people, making them sick. They can also try to chase away spirits that are causing trouble to the group. In addition to healing, the shaman uses his powers to try to influence the weather, the growth of crops, and success in battles with other groups. He is also called upon at times of birth, death, and initiation to see that rituals are properly observed.

Ceremonies and festivals are held for the spirits and to mark special events. On these occasions the people may wear garments made from bird feathers; necklaces made from seeds, shells, bones, and animal teeth; and ornaments in their ears and noses. They may also paint their faces and bodies with natural dyes. Music and dancing are an important part of such cere-

(Photo courtesy of the Brazilian Tourist Office)

monies. Musical instruments are made from the materials of the forest. Bone or bamboo are used to make pipes and flutes, animal skins become drums, and gourds are used to make maracas.

It is through these ceremonies, and through the stories told about the origins of the Indians and their history, that each generation passes down its beliefs and legends to the next.

Figure 32 (above) A Yaminahua Indian, the chief of a recently contacted group from the upper Manu River region, wearing traditional ornaments.

Figure 31 (above) Indians craft tools, weapons, and objects for worship out of materials found in the forest. They also make jewelry—ear decorations from toucan feathers, chains of seeds, and necklaces made out of the teeth of animals killed during the hunt.

Figure 33 (above) The way of life of Indian communities is changing. These children from the Peruvian Amazon are learning to read and write in the village school. Will the traditional skills and beliefs of their people eventually die out?

Age of the conquistadors

A divided world

In June 1494, Spain and Portugal agreed to divide between themselves whatever areas of the world were still to be "discovered" by Europeans. Portugal would have all land within 370 leagues (about 1250 miles) west of the Cape Verde Islands, which are located about 625 miles off the west coast of Africa. Outside this boundary all lands would belong to Spain. No thought was given to the people who may inhabit the lands they discovered.

Within a few years, a Spaniard named Alonso de Ojeda and an Italian named Amerigo Vespucci had reached the coast of Brazil. Ojeda sailed north, while Vespucci sailed south, discovering the mouth of the Amazon. The following year, in 1500, the Portuguese admiral Pedro Alvares Cabral also sighted the east coast of South America and claimed it for Portugal. These discoveries led to the arrival of Spanish *conquistadors* (soldiers and adventurers) such as Francisco Pizarro on the west coast of the continent. Pizarro fought against, and finally destroyed, the empire of the Incas. The interior of the South American continent was then seen as "ripe for exploration."

Figure 34 Francisco Pizarro, the Spanish conquistador who defeated the Incas, and opened South America to exploration from the west.

(Photo courtesy of Popperfoto)

Voyage of discovery

In 1541, two explorers, Gonzalo Pizarro (brother of Francisco) and Francisco de Orellana set out in separate parties from Quito (in present-day Ecuador) on a voyage of discovery, and to search for gold. Pizarro's party included 350 armed soldiers, 4000 Indians to carry weapons and supplies, 2000 pigs for food, and 2000 fighting dogs trained to attack Indians. After crossing the Andes, Pizarro descended into the rainforest where the thick vegetation slowed his progress. Orellana's party moved almost as slowly, hindered by frequent Indian attacks.

The two groups finally met up and struggled on together until they came to the Coca River. There they obtained 16 canoes from a group of Indians, and built a boat to carry the supplies, continuing their journey by river. On reaching the Napo River, Pizarro sent Orellana on ahead in the boat with provisions and some 60 men. Pizarro later returned to Quito empty-handed; Orellana, however, came across the mightiest river on Earth—the Amazon.

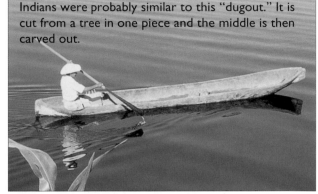

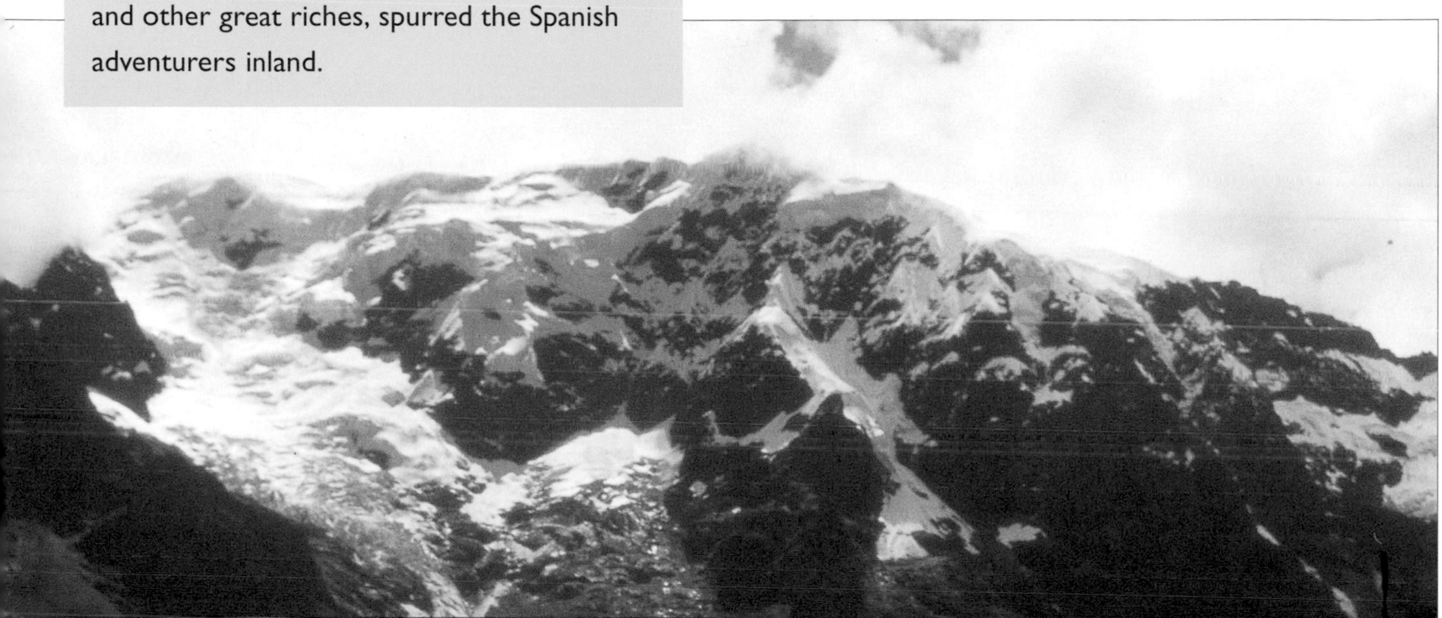

Figure 35 The canoes Pizarro obtained from the Indians were probably similar to this "dugout." It is cut from a tree in one piece and the middle is then carved out.

(Photo courtesy of Adventure World)

Indians captured by the Spanish had told of a forest kingdom called Manoa in which there was a great lake filled with gold. The kingdom was ruled over by "El Dorado"—the golden one—who was said to cover his naked body each day with gold dust. Visions of El Dorado, and other great riches, spurred the Spanish adventurers inland.

Figure 36 Gonzalo Pizarro's expedition into the Upper Amazon in search of gold was stopped by snow-capped mountain ranges such as these; on crossing the ranges, pouring rains frustrated their every effort. By the time Pizarro returned to Quito in August 1542 he was humiliated by his completely unsuccessful mission. He had found no gold, and of his original party only 70 Spanish soldiers remained. The other soldiers and Indians were lost to the rugged interior and the animals had died or been eaten.

(Photo courtesy of Destination Holidays)

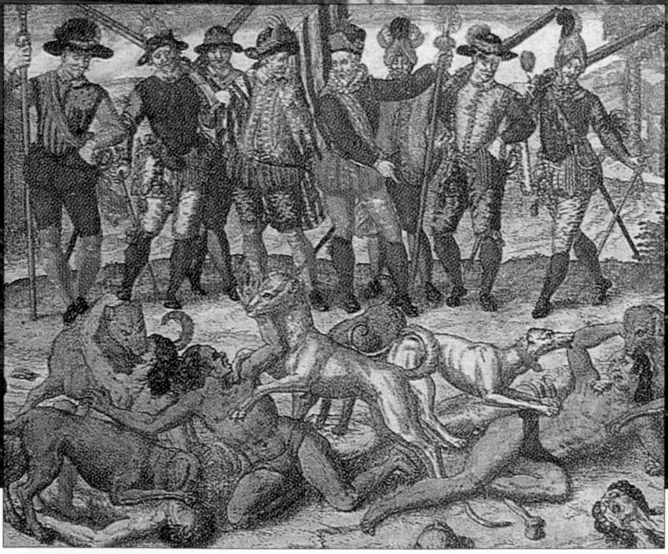

Figure 37 (above) Indians not already frightened by the Spaniards' horses were utterly terrified of their specially trained dogs. Pizarro took 2000 ferocious Indian-attacking dogs on his expedition.

(Engraving in Theodor de Bry, Historia Americae, *Frankfurt 1602.)*

Orellana's journey

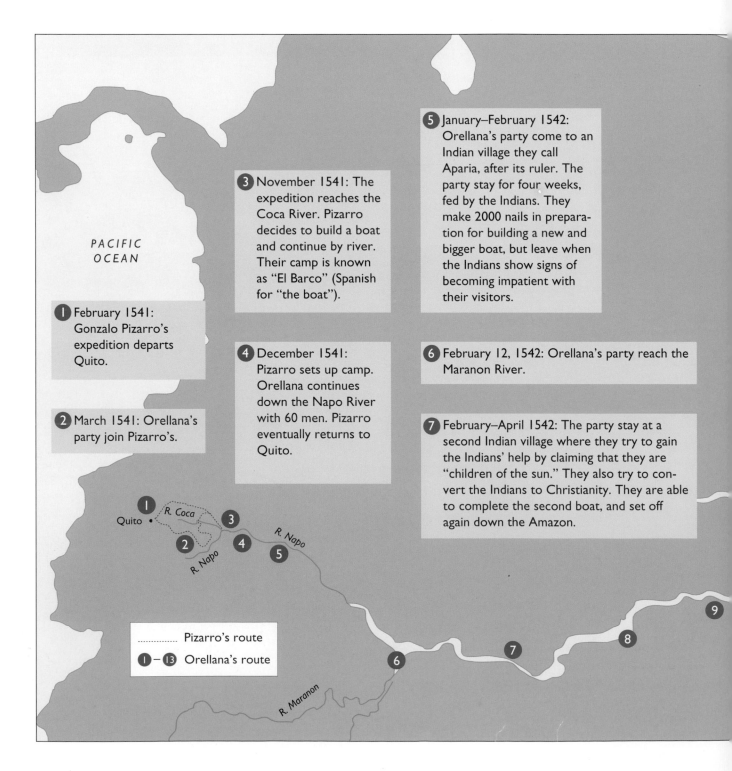

5 January–February 1542: Orellana's party come to an Indian village they call Aparia, after its ruler. The party stay for four weeks, fed by the Indians. They make 2000 nails in preparation for building a new and bigger boat, but leave when the Indians show signs of becoming impatient with their visitors.

3 November 1541: The expedition reaches the Coca River. Pizarro decides to build a boat and continue by river. Their camp is known as "El Barco" (Spanish for "the boat").

1 February 1541: Gonzalo Pizarro's expedition departs Quito.

4 December 1541: Pizarro sets up camp. Orellana continues down the Napo River with 60 men. Pizarro eventually returns to Quito.

6 February 12, 1542: Orellana's party reach the Maranon River.

2 March 1541: Orellana's party join Pizarro's.

7 February–April 1542: The party stay at a second Indian village where they try to gain the Indians' help by claiming that they are "children of the sun." They also try to convert the Indians to Christianity. They are able to complete the second boat, and set off again down the Amazon.

PACIFIC OCEAN

Quito

R. Coca

R. Napo

R. Napo

R. Maranon

·············· Pizarro's route

1 – **13** Orellana's route

Figure 38 Orellana's voyage of discovery down the Amazon, 1542.

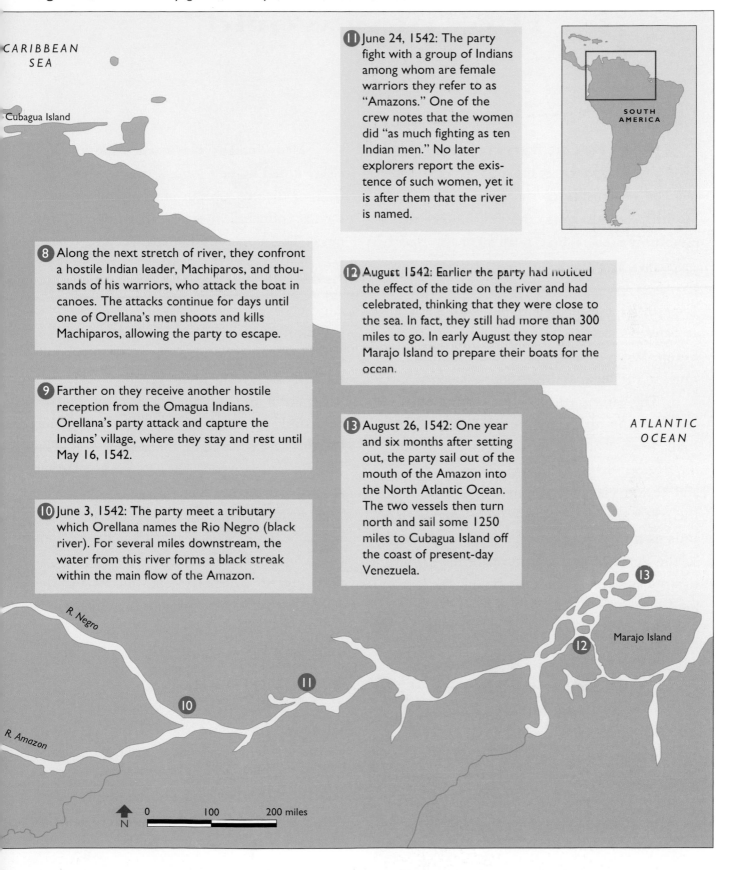

11 June 24, 1542: The party fight with a group of Indians among whom are female warriors they refer to as "Amazons." One of the crew notes that the women did "as much fighting as ten Indian men." No later explorers report the existence of such women, yet it is after them that the river is named.

8 Along the next stretch of river, they confront a hostile Indian leader, Machiparos, and thousands of his warriors, who attack the boat in canoes. The attacks continue for days until one of Orellana's men shoots and kills Machiparos, allowing the party to escape.

9 Farther on they receive another hostile reception from the Omagua Indians. Orellana's party attack and capture the Indians' village, where they stay and rest until May 16, 1542.

10 June 3, 1542: The party meet a tributary which Orellana names the Rio Negro (black river). For several miles downstream, the water from this river forms a black streak within the main flow of the Amazon.

12 August 1542: Earlier the party had noticed the effect of the tide on the river and had celebrated, thinking that they were close to the sea. In fact, they still had more than 300 miles to go. In early August they stop near Marajo Island to prepare their boats for the ocean.

13 August 26, 1542: One year and six months after setting out, the party sail out of the mouth of the Amazon into the North Atlantic Ocean. The two vessels then turn north and sail some 1250 miles to Cubagua Island off the coast of present-day Venezuela.

CARIBBEAN SEA

Cubagua Island

SOUTH AMERICA

ATLANTIC OCEAN

R. Negro

R. Amazon

Marajo Island

0   100   200 miles

N

The "new world"

Settlers, bandits, priests ...

On the other side of the continent to the Spanish conquistadors, the Portuguese were establishing their first settlement in Brazil called Sao Vicente, near present-day Sao Paulo. By 1549 there were 12 official areas (called "captaincies") in the new colony with a capital at Salvador. Settlers from the "old world" of Europe began to arrive, keen to make their fortunes in the "new world" of South America.

The early settlers stayed mainly by the coast, setting up trading posts where they initially traded in brazilwood, which was used for dyeing cloth in Europe. Then sugarcane and cotton plantations were established, and the Portuguese forced many unwilling Indians into slave labor. The Indians resisted, so the Portuguese began to bring in Africans to work as slaves. This "slave trade" was to last for 300 years.

Clash of cultures

"My Lord the King, my daughter the Princess, and my son the Prince ... shall see to it that these people [the Indians] are treated in a just and kindly fashion."

The words of the Last Will of Queen Isabella of Spain were, unfortunately, only words. The history of the Indian people of the Amazon region has been mainly one of suffering and injustice at the hands of European explorers, prospectors, and other settlers.

Many Indians who avoided slavery were either killed by new settlers who wanted their land, or died as a result of European diseases, such as influenza, to which they had no resistance. The remaining Indians retreated farther into the forest.

Landowners who were unable to obtain African slaves organized groups of *bandeirantes* (adventurers) who ventured deep into the forest to capture Indians. Often their targets were the missions set up by Jesuit priests. The Jesuits had braved the interior looking for Indians who could be converted to Christianity, but they had not counted on the bandeirantes. The Jesuit missions were eventually pushed farther south to escape the raids.

In the 1690s gold was discovered in Brazil, beginning a new industry in prospecting and mining, and bringing wealth to some settlers, but no benefits to the Indians. As the colony became richer, demands began for Brazil to become independent of Portuguese rule, something that was finally achieved in 1888.

... and scientists

As well as the settlers who continued to arrive in Brazil throughout the 1700s and 1800s, European scientists began to make the journey too, drawn by reports of the extraordinary rainforest and its plants, animals, and people.

In 1735, the French scientist Charles Marie de La Condamine was sent to South

(Photo courtesy of Destination Holidays)

Figure 39 (below) Among his discoveries in the Amazon during the 1840s, botanist Robert Schomburak found a giant waterlily almost 7 feet wide. Schomburk named it *Victoria regia*, in honor of England's queen.

Figure 40 British naturalist Henry Walter Bates spent 11 years exploring Amazonia, from 1848 to 1859. In all, he collected more than 14,000 specimens, mostly of insects, which he sold to museums. He published an account of his travels, including sketches of many plants and animals.

(Drawings from Henry Walter Bates's The Naturalist on the River Amazons, 1863 and 1892)

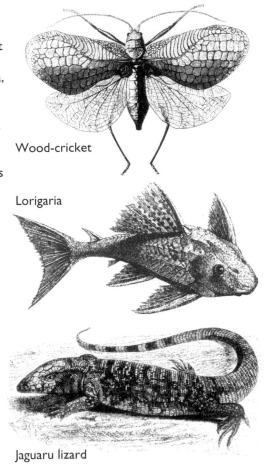

Wood-cricket

Lorigaria

Jaguaru lizard

Figure 41 (right) The rainforest still holds much mystery for science. Already compounds from the tropical rainforest are used to treat headaches and eye problems, and provide muscle-relaxing substances used in surgery. Scientists need more time to study the rainforest, but its rapid destruction could mean that they will be unable to discover other life-saving compounds.

(Photo courtesy of Destination Holidays)

America. He explored Amazonia and returned to France the following year with the first real scientific information about the region, including details of the poison curare used by the Indians, and the rubber tree. Some decades later, Baron Alexander von Humboldt, a German naturalist, and Aime Bonpland, a French botanist, spent five years exploring Amazonia. Bonpland collected and described some 6000 previously unknown species of plants. Other scientists followed in their footsteps, studying the region's unique flora and fauna.

The rubber revolution

Trees which produce rubber sap grow wild in Amazonia. Until the 1840s, however, there was not a great deal of use for rubber as it was difficult to work with. In 1844, an American inventor, Charles Goodyear, developed "vulcanization," a process which makes rubber stronger and more "stretchy." Then in 1887, while working on his 10-year-old son's tricycle, John Boyd Dunlop came up with the idea of using an inflatable rather than a solid rubber tire. Dunlop went into business producing inflatable tires for bicycles and cars, and the demand for rubber increased.

Thousands of people flocked to the Amazon region, hoping to make their fortunes as rubber growers. Huge fortunes were made by some individual farmers. Rough Amazonian settlements that had been small collections of shacks before the boom were suddenly transformed into cities, boasting buildings made of imported marble, and the latest fashions and luxuries from Europe. In Manaus, for example, business was conducted using gold coins instead of paper money, and some wealthy residents were able to send their laundry all the way to Paris to be washed and ironed.

Most rubber tappers were unable to share in this luxury. Rubber tapping was the job of poor settlers and Indians who often endured terrible conditions. The job involved cutting grooves in the bark of the rubber tree so the sap (or latex) could ooze out into cups hung under each cut. After it had hardened, the latex was taken to the city where it was made into rubber.

In the 1920s, the boom ended. Using seeds taken from Amazonia, the British started to grow rubber on plantations in Malaysia. Plantations made the trees easier to manage and the rubber cheaper to collect, eventually bringing the price of rubber down. In addition, after years of harvesting, the Amazonian rubber trees were producing less and less latex.

Rubber is still exported from Brazil today, but conditions have not changed and the tappers, who work hard to tap the latex from up to 80 trees a day, barely make a living.

The birth of rubber

An explorer who traveled up the Amazon River in the 1700s, Charles Marie de La Condamine, reported to the French Academy of Sciences in Paris: "A tree called *heve* grows in the province of Esmeraldas. With a single incision it secretes a milky-white fluid that gradually hardens and darkens on contact with air. The Mayan Indians call the resin obtained therefrom *cauchu*, which is pronounced *cahouchou* and means 'tree-that-weeps'." La Condamine had found the rubber tree.

Boom times in Manaus

While the rubber tappers underwent terrible hardships for very little payment, the wealthy rubber barons and residents of Manaus lived lavishly. Anything European was preferred. Although the Government tried to encourage crops such as cotton, rice, tobacco, and coffee, they were not cultivated, yet potatoes from Portugal, cauliflowers from Brussels, Danish butter, German sauerkraut, English sausage, and mortadella from Milan were all imported. The homes on fashionable streets were sumptuous two-story mansions built to the European pattern, with high ceilings, noble stairways and roofs crowned with classical statues, within trim green yards.

One rubber baron commissioned an American colonial-style mansion to house his racehorses. When it was completed, he was so impressed with the result that he moved into one wing. A newly appointed Governor disliked the half-completed Governor's palace so much that he authorised $12,000 worth of dynamite to blow it up.

The Opera House (above right) began as a $7200 project but eventually cost well over $800,000. Technicians and laborers were offered free passage from all over Europe. Its iron framework came from Glasgow and the 66,000 blue and gold tiles on its dome were imported from Alsace-Lorraine. One hundred crates of carved furniture were shipped from London. Carrara marble pillars soared in the foyer, as the 1600 patrons sat beneath Venetian glass chandeliers, illuminating angels and cherubs on the domed sky-blue ceiling. Even before the building was opened the Governor stated "When the growth of our city demands it, we'll pull down this opera house and build another."

Figure 42 (right) Rubber tapping, showing the latex oozing from the freshly cut groove into the collecting cup.

Figure 43 (below) In the "golden age" of Manaus, a grand Opera House was built which boasted performances from three different theater companies. Money made from rubber also paid for the running of electric trams in the city.

Photo courtesy of Coo-ee Picture Library)

(Photo courtesy of Ford Australia)

Figure 44 (above)   In 1888, John Dunlop developed the first air-filled tire. As a result of this, and the growing automobile industry, there was a massive increase in the demand for Amazonian rubber, leading to the great "rubber boom."

Four Amazonian towns

Much of the population of Amazonia live in rough towns and villages strung out along the rivers and roads. These settlements mainly consist of simple houses made from wood or adobe (mud brick) and stores selling basic supplies.

Larger towns attract industry and commerce, often related to rainforest products. As in the rest of Brazil, wealth and poverty exist side by side. Large numbers of poor people are constantly arriving in the towns when they find they can no longer survive in the rainforest. Four important centers in the Amazon Basin are Manaus, Belem, Iquitos, and Port Velho.

Manaus: city of free trade

The city of Manaus lies on the Rio Negro, close to where it joins the Amazon. Its population is over one million. Before the rubber boom, Manaus was a small town; rubber brought incredible prosperity, which is still evident in buildings such as the Opera House. After the boom, Manaus lost most of its wealth and its importance.

In the 1960s Manaus was made a free trade zone, which means that companies setting up business there do not have to pay tax. Many of the industries in Manaus make

Figure 45 Manaus is situated where the Rio Negro meets the Amazon. The city is an example of how industry is moving ever deeper into the Amazonian rainforest, threatening its precious resources.

and sell cheap electrical goods, and attract workers from all over Brazil.

Belem: port of Amazonia

With a population of over two million people, Belem is a different kind of center. In the old days it was known for the trading of slaves, cocoa, and spices. Now it is an industrial city and a port, situated where the Amazon River opens into the ocean. The two main rainforest products shipped from Belem are brazil nuts and timber.

Like Manaus, Belem benefited from the rubber boom—many substantial buildings dating from those times can still be seen in the city. However, unlike Manaus, Belem has good roads connecting it with the rest of the country.

The people of Belem reflect the different waves of settlers in Brazil over the centuries—

Figure 46 Once known as a center for trading slaves, cocoa, and spices, Belem is now known as a port supplying brazil nuts and timber.

Indian, Portuguese, African, and Japanese. Many of the inhabitants are either unemployed or work at very low-paid jobs. For such people, home is on a pavement or in the slums at the edge of the city.

Iquitos: a town in isolation

Located deep in the rainforest in the far east of Peru, Iquitos is the main town of the Upper Amazon. Its isolation means that Iquitos can only be reached by plane or boat. Ocean-going ships can travel up the river as far as Iquitos; beyond the town the waterway becomes too difficult to negotiate. This prosperous town, which also boomed with the rubber trade, is today the center for oil exploration in Peru. However, despite the prosperity of some citizens, a very large number still live in slum housing.

Figure 47 Tourism provides some jobs in the isolated town of Iquitos on the Peruvian Amazon.

Port Velho: the gold town

Gold has transformed this once small town on the Madeira River into a bustling city of nearly half a million people. In addition to gold mining, agricultural projects have also brought new residents and industry to the town.

Amazonians today

Today, Indians living the traditional way of life form a tiny minority of the population of Amazonia. Other Indians try to maintain some aspects of traditional life in the forest while also participating in the modern world. Yet others have completely lost the culture of their ancestors, and live in the towns where they often have to struggle to survive.

Another group who continue to depend on the forest are the *caboclas* (people of mixed Indian and Portuguese or Spanish heritage). The caboclas survive in much the same way as the Indians of previous centuries, using shifting cultivation, and living on what they can grow and on what the rainforest provides. Even among the caboclas, there are those who, by circumstance or choice, now live in or near towns and lead much more Westernized lives.

The largest number of people in the Amazon Basin are settlers who have arrived from the cities and elsewhere, hoping to start a new life by farming. Often they settle illegally by rivers or roads, and clear land to grow food and cash crops such as rice or coffee. Many of them fail because of poor soil, and are forced to move on to other land or into shanty towns. Not surprisingly, there has been conflict between the settlers and the Indians over the possession of land.

In earlier times Amazonia had very few roads, which meant that huge areas of rain-

(Photo courtesy of Peregrine Adventure)

Figure 48 (above)   At Porto Escadaria dos Remedios, these shanty huts, all too typical in South America, are a reminder of the poverty that is unfortunately part of the lives of many Amazonians today.

forest remained relatively untouched. However, in recent years the Brazilian Government has commissioned huge road-building projects through rainforest areas. One such road is the Trans-Amazon Highway, which spans the country from east to west. Over 3000 miles long, it was built to exploit the mineral wealth

(Photo courtesy of Adventure World)

Figure 49 (right) The Trans-Amazon Highway cuts a swathe through the rainforest. Clearing the vegetation has led to problems of erosion.

Figure 50 (below)   Many Indians have combined aspects of traditional and Western lifestyles. Here an Auca Indian shows two visitors around parts of the Amazonian rainforest of Ecuador.

(Photo courtesy of Peregrine Adventure)

of Amazonia, and to provide faster transportation of goods. Unfortunately the road cut right through the rainforest, destroying thousands of trees. During heavy rains, sections are actually washed away, causing erosion and silting of streams.

The Brazilian Government hoped that by building these roads, settlers would be encouraged to open up the region, leading to jobs and prosperity. Unfortunately, this has not happened. Despite offers of cheap or free housing and land, settlers have not arrived in huge numbers as expected. As a result, the government is struggling to pay back the enormous international loans taken out to build the roads.

Industries in Amazonia

Today, the rainforest is threatened by a number of different industries. Although there may be laws and regulations prohibiting activities that damage the environment or force Indians from their land, these are often not enforced.

Ranching

In the last 15 years or so, the raising of beef cattle on huge ranches has become a major industry in the Amazon Basin. Three-quarters of the land that is cleared of rainforest is used for this purpose. Such intensive grazing reduces the land, which is not fertile in the first place, to dust. The ranchers or graziers then need more land, which they force small farmers to sell to them. The beef produced mainly goes to supply fast-food chains in the U.S.A.

(Photo courtesy of Adventure World)

Figure 51 (above)   The spread of industry into Amazonia has led to the construction of the Trans-Amazon Highway to carry timber, cattle, and iron ore.

Logging

Commercial logging is the second biggest cause of destruction of the forests. Some harvested wood is used locally for firewood and charcoal. Much fine wood, particularly hardwood like mahogany, is exported, especially to Japan and western Europe. Other woods are exported as wood chips and plywood. Industrialized nations participate in the destruction of the rainforest by importing these products.

Even when loggers only want one specific type of forest tree, many of the surrounding trees are usually destroyed in the process. Others are destroyed when access roads are made through the forest. Little or no replanting is taking place.

Mining

Amazonia is rich in resources such as manganese, oil, aluminum, diamonds, and tin. It also holds the greatest deposits of iron ore in the world. A lot of heat is needed to smelt the mined ore, and this is produced by burning firewood. Although regulations insist that only trees taken from reforested plantations be used, in practice the wood is often taken from virgin forest.

Amazonia is also mined for gold. There are up to one million gold miners in the region, who prospect by digging and using dredges. Mining companies destroy the rain-

Figure 52 (left) Another industry affecting Amazonia is tourism. If tourism is managed responsibly, the region can be visited without causing significant harm. However, care must be taken to ensure that tourist traffic, such as the river boat shown here, does not damage the precious environment.

Figure 53 (right) Amazonia is not the only region in Brazil under threat. Spread over 15,000 square miles, the Pantanal is the largest inland swamp in the world. However, clearing of the land for soybean plantations has led to silting. This has damaged the plant life and threatens the survival of animals, birds, and the swamp itself.

forest by cutting down trees to set up mines. Although it is illegal, mines often use mercury (a highly poisonous substance) to extract the gold, and waste mercury ends up in the river system.

Dams

Its huge volume of water makes the Amazon River system ideal for hydroelectric schemes. An extensive series of dams is planned for the region—124 over the next 15 years—to provide Brazil with cheap electricity. Many thousands of acres of rainforest will have to be destroyed and flooded to build the dams, and half a million people will lose their homes and livelihoods. In addition, the dams will also provide a breeding ground for mosquitoes, which carry malaria.

Cocaine

The drug cocaine is another threat to the rainforest. In the old days, Indians used to chew the leaves of the coca plant as a mild stimulant. Now farmers grow coca as a cash crop, clearing tracts of virgin rainforest and using harmful herbicides to do so. The Brazilian Government is trying to stamp out the growing of coca, but it remains a multimillion dollar industry.

Fightback and the future

Amazonia is one of the most incredible places on Earth. Since European settlement began in the 1500s, however, the Indian way of living with the forest has been replaced by the idea that the forest is something for people to plunder. In recent years the value of the Amazon has begun to be recognized. Today there are many individuals and organizations, both inside and outside Brazil, working toward trying to save the remaining treasures of the region.

Some organizations working for change have been formed by the indigenous people who are at last starting to make their voices heard. They are fighting back. Some of them have demanded, for instance, that gold prospectors and others compensate them for digging up their land. Rubber tappers, Indians, and others who live in the forest have also formed alliances to challenge governments and big business over the way they are treated. As they are few in number and have very little representation in parliament, it is still difficult for these people to make an impression.

Champion of the rainforest

Perhaps the best-known person to work toward saving the rainforest was Chico Mendes (Francisco Mendes Filho). He grew up in Amazonia, in a home that was a wooden shack in a forest clearing, and worked as a rubber

(Photo courtesy of the Brazilian Tourist Office)

tapper. He was angered by the fact that timber companies were rapidly cutting down rainforest trees, destroying the rubber trees as they did so. The cleared land was then sold to cattle ranchers.

His attempts to combat logging turned Chico Mendes into an activist. He not only organized thousands of rubber tappers into a union to speak out against the timber companies, he also fought against the mining and

Figure 54 (below) Concerned Brazilians and others from all over the world are beginning to draw attention to the urgent need to protect the wilderness of Amazonia and its peoples.

Figure 55 (left) Indians have begun to fight back, demanding fair treatment, land rights, voting rights, and the chance to preserve their culture and traditions.

(Photo courtesy of Destination Holidays)

(Photo courtesy of Adventure World)

Figure 56 (above right) Industries such as ranching, logging, and mining create jobs, but they also create problems for the river and rainforest, and for its human and animal inhabitants.

road- and dam-building activities that were harming the forest.

Chico became well known around the world for his efforts to make people aware of the damage that was being done. He was very successful in gaining attention, and because of this was seen as a danger by some. In 1988, he was shot dead by cattle ranchers who found him too threatening to their plans, but others have taken his place and continue to speak out.

In June 1988, the New Constitution of Brazil acknowledged: "the social structure, languages, beliefs, and traditions of Indians are hereby recognized, as are their natural rights to lands they have traditionally occupied." However, that same document still made no allowance for Indians to vote.

The message

Chico Mendes's message, and that of the other rainforest activists, is that the forest can be useful to Brazilians without being destroyed in the process. The Indians have much to teach us about how the forest can be treated with respect. They have shown it is possible to harvest the nuts, fruit, oils, spices, dyes, fish, and medicinal plants without harming their habitat. Modern technology may also be harnessed to provide alternative methods of farming that do not harm the river or the land.

1992 Earth Summit

In 1992, an Earth Summit was held in Rio de Janeiro, one of Brazil's major cities. Representatives from over 150 countries attended, and discussed environmental issues. Many countries found they had common problems. Although not a great deal of action has come out of the summit, awareness was raised, and the next summit could see more definite action to conserve resources such as the Amazon rainforest.

(Photo courtesy of Destination Holidays)

Figure 57 Sunset over the Amazon – a wilderness worth preserving for future generations.

Glossary

Amazonia The region that comprises the Amazon River and its basin.

caboclas People who are of mixed Indian and either Portuguese or Spanish heritage.

conquistador A Spanish soldier/adventurer. Conquistadors arrived on the west coast of South America in the 1500s.

curare A poison made from plant extracts.

deforestation The clearance of forests over a wide area.

ecology The branch of biology that deals with the way living things relate to each other and to their environment.

ecosystem The interconnected web of plant and animal life that survives in a particular environment.

environment Physical surroundings.

epiphyte Plant which grows on another plant but does not take water or minerals from it.

flora and fauna The Latin terms for plants and animals.

glacier A slowly moving river of ice.

Gondwana A "supercontinent" that probably existed up until 160 million years ago. It consisted of what are now Australia, Africa, South America, India, Antarctica, and New Zealand.

habitat The area in which a plant or animal naturally lives; its home.

igapo A type of rainforest found in the Amazon region that is flooded during the wet season.

indigenous Original (people, animals, or plants) of an area.

savanna A grassy plain with few or no trees.

sediment Small particles of matter carried by a river.

shaman A male member of an Indian group who conducts special ceremonies, and is thought to be able to communicate with spirits.

silt Fine mud or clay carried by a river.

species A group of plants or animals that have some common features, and can breed with one another.

terra firma A type of rainforest found in Amazonia. It is characterized by taller trees.

tidal Having daily tides, like the sea.

tributary A river flowing into a main river.

varzea The part of a forest that is flooded for several months at a time, such as that growing along the edge of a river.

virgin forest Untouched area of forest.

vulnerable Unprotected; able to be hurt or damaged.

Index

alligators (*see* caymans)

Amazonia

climate 7

geography 4–7, 10–11

geology 8

Amazons (female warriors) 33

anacondas 13, 18–19

Andes Mountains 4, 8, 10, 30

animals 12–15 (*see also* names of specific animals)

preservation 17

armadillos 13

Bates, Henry Walter 35

Belem 5, 11, 38–39

birds 12–13, 16–17

Bonpland, Aime 35

Brazil 4, 5, 6, 7, 25, 36, 38, 40, 44–45

Cabral, Pedro Alvares 30

caimans 18–19

capybaras 13, 14–15

cattle industry 42

cocaine 43

conquistadors 30–33

curare 27, 35

dams 43, 45

El Dorado 31

environmental issues 20–23, 44–46

Europeans

explorers 30–33

priests 34

scientists 34–35

settlers 34–35, 40–41

fish 14–15

Gondwana 8

Humboldt, Alexander von 35

Indians 5, 7, 24–29

beliefs and spirituality 17, 28–29, 31

contact with Europeans 30–35

farming and crops 21, 26–27

lifestyle 24–25, 40–41, 44–45

prehistory 8–9

Iquitos 4, 10, 38–39

La Condamine, Charles Marie de 35, 36

macaws 13, 16–17

Manaus 4, 11, 36–38

Marajo Island 11, 33

Mendes, Chico 44–46

mining industry 42–43, 44

monkeys 15

Obidos 11

Odeja, Alonso de 30

Orellana, Francisco de 30–33

Peru 4, 6, 8, 10, 24, 38

Pizarro, Francisco 30

Pizarro, Gonzalo 30–32

Port Vehlo 4, 11, 38–39

rainforest 5, 6, 8

conservation 44–46

destruction 17, 22–23, 40, 41, 44–46

ecosystem 12–13, 20–23

medicinal plants 20–21, 35

rivers

Apurimac 4, 10

Branco 11

Coca 30, 32

Ene 10

Japura 10

Madeira 4, 7, 11, 39

Maranon 4, 10, 32

Napo 10, 30, 32

Negro 4, 11, 33, 38

Para 11

Purus 10

Putumayo 4

Solimoes 4, 10

Tocantins 11

Tombo 10

Trombetas 11

Ucayali 4, 10

rubber 35, 36–37, 38, 39, 44

slash and burn farming 26–27

slavery 34, 36, 38, 39

tapirs 13

timber industry 22, 38, 39, 42, 44

toucans 13, 16–17

tourism 39, 43

Trans-Amazon Highway 4–5, 41, 42

Vespucci, Amerigo 30